I0132604

THE
COMPLETE POETRY
OF
NORMAN A.J. BERISFORD

L.R. Price Publications Ltd

i

Published 2016 by L.R. Price Publications Ltd.

L.R. Price Publications Ltd,

27 Old Gloucester Street,

London, WC1N 3AX.

www.lrpricepublications.com

ISBN: 0992903718
ISBN-13: 978-0-9929037-1-8

DEDICATION

TO MARGARET WITH LOVE

THE COMPLETE POETRY OF NORMAN A.J. BERISFORD

CONTENTS

ACKNOWLEDGEMENTS

The publisher would like to thank the following people:
Matthew Vidler, Lorraine Price, Leonard West and Susan
Woodard for their advice, hard work and support, without which
this book would not have been published.

The publisher would also like to acknowledge
www.pixabay.com for providing the cover artwork.

The author would like to thank the following people:
Paul Trieu; Nigel Goodman; John Morris; and of course
Margaret Berisford; for their support and encouragement.

The author would also like to acknowledge Frederick Forsyth
for his story The Shepherd (Published by Hutchinson, 1975); and
Edward Thomas for his poem Adlestrop (Published in 1917); for
the inspiration for his poems by the same name..

THE COMPLETE POETRY OF NORMAN A.J. BERISFORD

9

AS CREATION CAME

Beauty was by fire and thunder as creation came,
   In strength and tenderness - both the same;
The Earth's crust melting and then glowing,
   And then only God the future knowing.

Where is the sun to give us all the light,
   Then reflecting on the moon at night?
Then warmth to set the seeds,
   Giving earthly creatures all their needs.

The oceans and the land proclaimed,
   With order made and beauty tamed,
A portion of this wonderous sphere,
   Share the seasons of each new year.

Then, followed soon the herbage green,
   And animals, birds and creatures.
Now, fishes in the deep blue sea,
   In God's Creation for all to see.

ELEGY

Hello my love, it's wonderful to have you near,
Come closer darling, I can hardly hear.

What joy it was on Woodbury Hill,
　　Just two of us laughing, what a thrill.

Please pass the water darling, I need a drink,
　　Oh, that's better now, and I only think.

Of all the times my eyes were dancing,
　　Yet with you my sweet, hardly chancing.
Do you remember the day we wed?
　　Just before Christmas, I'm sure you said.
So secretly a dream come true,
　　My only love forever, just with you.

Would you please pull up the sheet,
　　That is so kind of you, my sweet.

Walking through the clouds and early dew,
　　In Worcestershire, where we loved and knew.
And hiding our secret love each day,
　　Just you and me, with hearts so gay.

I'm sorry darling. but I feel unwell,
And what it is, is hard to tell.

I now know what in life you missed,
   With me, who hardly ever kissed.
But, my sweet, I kissed you every day,
   With my heart and soul, that was my way.

Oh darling, would you call a nurse for me,
   As I feel so unwell. and can hardly see.

Please squeeze my hand my darling dear,
   I feel that time is drawing near.
Goodbye my love, my darling love,
   Till we meet again in the world above.

THE MORNING WALK

Every morning just at dawn,
　Another day for me is born;
Just to walk in God's fresh air,
　Without worry and without care.

I leave the house just after seven,
　And look with joy drenched eyes - this heaven;
Of man and nature's arts so bold,
　With homes and gardens, young and old.

My first great pleasure, might I say,
　Is where my love and I do stay;
And then to my surprise, a tower,
　Where perhaps some gallant held his power.

And then I clumber up the street,
　Past bungalows - so small, so sweet;
And glancing to my left I see
　Some towering houses, one, two three.

But onward, onward, would I lurch,
　Past cottages and so to church;
But no my meandering cannot stay,
　Except to feast my eyes along the way.

Now on my right, an ancient hill,
　　Now changed by tree and daffodil;
Where once the languid cows would graze,
　　In starlit nights and summer days.

And now I stop and turn my gaze,
　　To see the valley in morning haze;
With two great cherry trees so high,
　　With blossoms reaching to the sky.

What is this? Another tower?
　　A barbican to impress with power;
But surely not a castle gate,
　　For there's no castle - it's much too late.

But, well it could be guarding still,
　　Arley house upon the hill;
Looking eastward to greet the sun,
　　Each morning, that is yet begun.

And now the lawns so manicured,
　　For Mr. Public to be lured;
And sure enough it looks that way,
　　As here I pause, and long to stay.

Then, looking to the west I saw
　　The gatehouse and its open door;
The arboretum's fine display,
　　Yet all to see, one has to pay.

The cattle grid I leave behind,
 And in the park what should I find;
But random trees, and lambs and sheep,
 Some grazing still, while others sleep.

And now each morning still I find,
A loss as Park and Naboth is left behind;
 And forced now my progress woed,
 Drifting now upon the open road.

Now to my right I amble down,
 The tarmac's black and ample crown;
To stop and take just one more look,
 At bridge and valley of Kettle Brook.

Up from the valley so I strode
 Upon this dull and open road;
But now I see of yesteryear
 Home Farm and Laundry Cottage near.

What joy to see the Orchard new,
 Where Jersey cattle ruminate and chew;
And now the junction to my right
 Sees Forge Cottage in my flight.

Now weaving slowly back to home,
 Past school and parish rooms, as yet alone;
The bank is steep beneath the trees,
 As down I stride with care and ease.

Now suddenly, I find this gift from heaven,
    That lovely friend and neighbor: River Severn;
As home and garden is now won,
    And me to finish where I begun.

ADLESTROP

Yes, I'll tell you more of Adlestrop,
  On that June afternoon;
And why the train just had to stop,
  Not too late and not too soon.

It was a technical affair,
  As water fed the greedy engine;
With passengers quite unaware,
  Sitting there - no apprehension.

Edward Thomas idly dozing unaware,
  Was feeling fit to drop;
When suddenly he became aware,
  The train had stopped at Adlestrop.

It wasn't that he knew the place -
  He didn't care a jot;
It was that sign, face to face,
  That just read *"Adlestrop"*.

And in the silence, giving way,
  To country sounds of pure delight;
Two shorthorns lazing through the day,
  With flanks sunlit, rusty in the light.

Two blackbirds sing a roundelay,
   Chinking through the meadowsweet;
The willow-herb so pink, so gay,
    And all the birds of Cotswold sound so sweet.

And now, would you have ever guessed,
   But for that unscheduled stop;
The train, the passengers and all the rest,
    Would have never heard of Adlestrop.

To the memory of Edward Thomas.

THE MUSICIAN

If music be the… Oh, I've heard that one,
    Yes, indeed, not just once but by the ton;
When piano practice becomes a chore,
    The less I learn, and what is more.
My teacher says for her, it's just not fun.

Perhaps a trombone could be my fayre,
    And with my skill, extend my flair;
With my keyboard thrown away,
    I'd blow my heart out and give sway,
To rousing blast of striking air.

But what would my neighbors think? If so I chose,
    To play my flute just with my nose.
Or should I learn the violin,
    To chase them out with such a din,
That all the street would have to close.

Well, maybe with second thoughts I'll find,
    Some other instrument that's more than kind,
To those with ears attuned to hear,
    Such music that Handel would hold dear,
And leave all that cacophony behind.

JUST ONE YEAR

As January heralds a new year,
  Thou winter in the garland Janus shares,
With catkins, aconites and snowdrops,
  Dressed up to display their winter wears.

As February proclaims itself with gorse,
  And Candlemas is upon us once again,
The willow catkins delight the eye,
  Through all of winters fog and rain.

With periwinkles, daffodils and violets,
  The winds advance the god of Mars,
Braving each new day with hopes of spring,
  With frosty nights beneath the stars.

The bluebells, cowslips and primroses,
  Give Graecian thoughts on opening of spring,
Each flower, the eye to wonder,
  As April lends the heart to sing.

Oh apple blossom, buttercup and hawthorn,
  Mother Mercury, what will you bring this day?
The sun in all its glory,
  To blind us with their bold display.

Delighting on this midsummer's day,
    Juno honours us with broom and roses,
With foxgloves, ferns and daises,
    As this month of June and colour sadly closes.

As water lily and meadowsweet do blossom,
    Caesar entreats us with hearts so gay,
As bumblebees their pollen bring,
    To nature's gift on this July day.

As poppies red and heather braving,
    Sweet August has arrived with chilly dew,
And such cool nights, that Augustus
    In his Roman empire had but few.

Oats, thistle-seed and dewstrung stumble.
    Mark September as nature's harvest time,
With chestnuts, juniper and blackberry,
    As thoughts of winter, autumn brings the sign.

Hazel-nuts and acorns, crab-apples and the sloe;
    October birds and squirrels busy meeting,
With elderberry, dogwood and hawthorn
    On the menu , feasting, feasting, feasting.

Seed vessels of cows-parsnip, dock an d willow,
    Blow free to brighten next year's spring.
As all November's yellow leaves have fallen,
    It sets the hearts in thanks to sing.

The privet, the holly and ivy
   Greet the bright December morn,
With mistletoe to share our love
   With that day our Lord was born.

MEDITATION

A radiant night - the lane bathed in light,
   And the wind is stilled, and lighter, flaccid,
      Walk my faltering steps as frost did bite.

How long must I, throughout the silent night waking,
   Just now as dark comes, night's soft shadows trailing,
      See you just once again, my long forsaking,
        As all is silent, now the vision failing.

When in my arms your slender form, trembling,
   And that smile upon your face that said,
So many words of so long remembering,
   But all is silent now, the lone voice, dead.

TEMPLEMEADS

Yes, I remember Templemeads,
    For I was there at Templemeads,
In July, not for long,
    Perhaps one half-hour or so.

Outside the cars and taxis,
    Were rumbling and grumbling,
For their treasured place,
    Between the cycle rack and the flower seller.

The July sun was burning down onto the,
    Goodbye streets, buildings and monuments,
In a kaleidoscope of golden haze,
    Shimmering and waving a farewell.

My blind eyes seeing everything, yet seeing nothing,
    I walked into the cool shadow of this,
Great cathedral of steam and locomotion,
    Waiting for the train taking me away.

Carrying a love letter in my pocket,
    Which I feared yet to open,
Sitting lonely in my carriage going away.
    Oh yes, I remember Templemeads.

TREES

Hearts of oak are our ships, so the poets say,
    And such majesty still reigns,
To remind us on each new day,
      That our love of England never wanes.

Now when we talk of magic, the ash,
    Is doubtless quite profound,
As warts and stitches and the rash,
    Once touched, are never found.

The alder prefers half-dry, half-water,
    In marshes and by rivers too,
And clogs were made that didn't falter,
    While charcoal made gunpowder too.

The beechwood in the Chiltern hills,
    Sustained the craftsman, without tire,
And, there, loftiness engenders thrills,
    Yet logs of beech sustained, Victoria's Palace fires.

The melting ice proclaimed the birch,
    As perhaps the first tree on this earth -
There's a little need to start a search,
    For it is certain of its worth.

The Stone Age man's food was very rare,
     And from the hazel, the nuts he chose,
To satisfy his meagre fayre,
  God's gift it was to ease his woes.

Oh, boxwood on the Surrey hill,
  So shy to show its crumpled form,
Is sheltered from the sun, as still,
  The beech trees shade, to keep it warm.

The holly defends itself with armour so severe,
  That it has no need to extend its height,
From the greed of cattle and of deer,
    With spikey leaves so green and bright.

When you know it, then you'll love it,
  The very best friend of mine;
As builders deal, they surely covet,
   Our native tree: the Scots pine.

The poisonous leaves do tell of yew,
  Yet monuments of men and sheltered groves,
Still share most English churchyards too,
  But yet so few, not seen in droves.

The Romans brought the chestnut to our land,
  Now seen roasting in our London streets,
With recipes simple and yet so grand,
  And once ground as meal in religious feasts.

The Worcester weed - the elm, I know,
    Hedge patterned in the Midland Plains,
Were feeding cattle long ago,
    Through summer's fires and winter's rains.

Who could be more pretty in this month of May,
    But the May-queen crowned with blossoms white,
With hawthorn and its bright display,
    That shines the day and shines the night.

The hornbeam, the horny tree, do grow,
    In counties close to London,
The most native of all the tress we know,
    And casts the shade as beech has done.

The common lime or linden as from Holland came,
    With avenues planted everywhere,
And as important as the tulip just the same,
    In parks and gardens, fine and fair.

Such winds blow the winged fruit everywhere,
    As brilliant autumn colours are aglow,
And the maple with its leaves so fair,
    The next year's harvest, here to sow.

Dutch clogs and doors and floors are best,
    From Poplar's straightened grain,
And shelters, screens and all the rest,
    That only good design could gain.

The rowan or the mountain ash, also known as the witchen,
    Is much beloved for its blossomed scent,
And protection from the witches, in church, in home and kitchen,
    No matter from where such ghouls were sent.

When Zacchaeus watched Christ's journey on his way,
    The sycamore enfolded him with care,
And noblemen from the precious day,
    Have their estates shaded good and fair.

LOVE IN THE SUN

A cloudless sky is fast approaching,
    Saying farewell to the day of gloom,
The clouds scudding by, no longer encroaching,
    With the sun, full of warmth, coming soon.

Will this be the day I've been waiting to see,
    With your eyes that I love, flash and flame,
And the warmth of your body recumbent with me,
    That nought in this world I could name.

With the sun burning down, time is dissolved,
    Our hearts melting and conjoined as one,
As if nothing in this world ever evolved,
    Except for our love, and the welcoming sun.

DREAMS

Dreams are but another life we live,
   Unbounded by our schemes;
As everything in life we give,
    But for the gift of dreams.

So dreams are not always remembered,
   Of things and people from our past;
But imagination, surely rendered,
    For just that moment, not to last.

Who is this pretty girl enticing me to love?
   And with unbridled passion I embrace her;
As warm I am in endless bliss.
   The dream is gone, and lost forever.

In dreams sometimes the past is told,
   Of things that were best forgot;
As memories of the past unfold,
  That sadly remind us of our lot.

I sometimes wake from a dream at night,
   And sweating fit to drown;
What is this that gives such a fright
   As I hide beneath the eiderdown?

The towering, gothic sandstone hall,
   Has beckoned me I feel;
That I should have to call,
Yet now is made of tinted glass and steel.

I travel through a town I know,
    Yet never seen before;
On foot, on bicycle, and in a car as though,
    Not once, not twice, but three or four times more.

Sitting in a concert hall,
   That I have been in many times before;
Then suddenly, I fall - I fall,
    To be landed on my office floor.

And now, in my thoughts of dreams,
   I often ponder why;
I'm always so confused it seems,
    Of life that goes awry.

THE CHANCE ENCOUNTER

I liked *that girl* - an angel passing by,
    Each morning, prompt at nine;
I wondered, would she look my way,
  Oh yes, perhaps in time.

Was it by chance she stopped that morning,
 That morning just at nine;
With trembling heart, I said: "Hello,
    I'd love to see you". She said "Fine".

It was a foursome at the George,
 "I'll bring my friend," said she;
And there, together, just to chat,
    From two till half-past three.

Four strangers to be meeting now,
    Words stuttered to and fro,
A whispered date I sought, but
    Not with *that girl* I know.

Two minds, entwined forever,
  As from that whisper came;
A love, a joy and friendship,
    That life can never wane.

Years fall like leaves in life,
In gently rushing wings,
And all that happiness we live,
Wishing for a thousand springs.

THE SHEPHERD

Christmas eve, sitting in my cockpit,
    With the Vampire's engines purring low;
Waiting for the tower to clear me,
    And restless for the call to go.
The Royal Airforce base in Germany,
    Had been my home for Christmas fifty-seven;
But chance has let me return home,
    To family and friends, thank heaven.

The runway's thin white line and burning lights,
    "Charlie Delta - clear to take off." On my way;
Easing the throttle forward, she takes to the air,
    The nose now rising and clearing the runway.
Pulling the Vampire into a climbing turn,
    To my left, wheels and undercarriage locked;
I leave the runway and switch to channel D,
    While climbing at a speed of knots.

Checking channel D, then over the Dutch coast,
    And, after some minutes' flying time, change to channel F;
To call Lakenheath, to give me a steer;
    Then, in fourteen minutes more, I think of my Christmas roast.
No problems - sixty minutes flying time and, with ease,
    The descent to landing - just eighty minutes in the air;
My electric compass settled on a course for home,
    And four hundred miles to Lakenheath, without a care.

Now thinking of my Christmas leave to come,
   And a lift from Lakenhean to London, then back home,
My mind excited for my family and fun.
   Then some minutes over the North Sea, my headphone,
Becomes silent, and knowing that something's not right,
   I glance at my compass and feel alone.
No longer on my setting, but spinning, what a fright!
   But I know ground-control approach will guide me home.

Knowing the correct procedure, I click to channel D,
   "Charlie Delta, Charlie Delta - calling Beveland control."
Oh, my God - I fear I'm now in such a hole.
   Switching to channel F - the radio just as dead,
Feeling very lonely in the sky this winter's night;
   No contact, just hurtling through the air as dark as lead.
But I must compose myself: no pain - no fright,
   As procedure learned go through my head.

Procedure to stay alive is always in one's training,
   And, now I must do my very best.
Compass and radio gone, with both circuits failing;
   The main fuse blow out I confirm by my test.
Reducing airspeed setting will give me flight endurance.
   The altimeter and airspeed indicator, only now left,
Means I only know how high and how fast that I'm flying,
   But at least that does afford me some sort of assurance.

It's easy landing an aircraft by visual means,
In daylight, but in darkness one only sees,
The lights of towns, motorways and lighting beams,
And other such illuminations with ease.
I thought now that the North Sea could swallow me,
I feel so lonely, and fear the most,
That no one would ever know - just me and the sea;
A cruel finish from my watery host.

Now at low level, and all that I could see,
Were clouds of an endless sea of white;
Which could only be the east Anglican fog,
And that's impossible to navigate at night.
I could not overfly the fog to the westward,
In unfamiliar country - that could not be right;
And with my fuel low, that could not be good,
The situation now is very far from bright.

At ten-thousand feet, and with nought to see,
I must stay airborne and, without an ejector seat;
I would have to bail out over the North Sea,
And this procedure, in a Vampire, is no small feat.
Aircraft approaching Britain are visible on radar,
So, to draw their attention I fly triangles, left and right;
Hoping for someone to see me, so far,
In this impossible situation, in the night.

Above the Norfolk fog, the triangle I kept flying,
With only ten minutes flying time left, I must be seen;
I'm so worried now that I could soon be dying,
Why don't you see me on your radar screen?
Then, suddenly, below my wing tip I saw a shadow,
Of another aircraft by me, keeping station,
But, going faster than this aircraft - I must now,
Apply my airbrakes, reducing speed, what elation!

And then he came towards me, his black bulk,
Showing against the white sheet of fog,
I could see two propellers and its shining hulk,
A De Havilland Mosquito, I remember from a log.
And from this Mosquito I could see a muffled head,
And goggles as he took a look right at me,
I nodded - pointed to my control panel that read:
LOW FUEL, then crossed my throat for him to see.

We were now heading down into the fog and,
I again used my airbrakes, and throttled down to keep;
This God-sent shepherd beside me. But where to land?
And still going down two thousand feet.
I then saw the letters *J K* painted on his plane,
And still descending gently, we went into a turn.
For God's sake - I'm running out of fuel, and its plain,
I have only three minutes left - nothing else to burn.

Then, suddenly, he straightened out and,
I almost lost him, But then I saw;
His flash dive signal with his left hand,
Then we dropped into a fog bank and for,
Some moments I followed, into a flat descent,
Just a few hundred feet towards nothing - just free.
And with no visibility yet the Mosquito went
Flying with certainty, at something I could not see.

All of a sudden I saw lights and a streak of white paint,
And I closed down the power and held her steady;
The Vampire settled, and *bang* - we've landed and faint,
Then another bang, as we touched down and ready,
I then touched the brakes on, and the nose slammed down;
Then, to my left, I saw the Mosquito roar past,
And I saw a flash of the pilot's hand to the crown.
At all, that sight of him would be my last.

I stepped from my cockpit at the call of a voice –
"Just jump in the car and well go to the mess,"
He said; "Without radio and compass you had no choice."
I said that I must have been guided in - no more or no less.
"We have no ground approach control," he said,
"No navigation equipment, not even a beacon.
And without lights you would surely be dead.
But come join us for supper through we have just eaten."

I then asked: "Why did you switch the runway lights on?"
And he said he heard a plane circling and making a din;
"You have landed just five miles from Cromer, at Minton -
It must have been a weather squadron that brought you in."
This guy Joe said that he had been at Minton for twenty years -
From just two years before the war, and all the rest.
 I asked "Who is the pilot in that picture, in all his gear?"
"It's Mr. Kavanagh, Sir, in the war and he was the best."

"He flew Pathfinder Mosquitos throughout the war,
And initials J K were marked on his plane.
And, without hesitation, because that was his law;
Shepherding lost pilots - that was his game:
Going to crippled planes and bringing them to Minton.
He was just superb - at the top of the tree!"
"Is he still doing it now?"- asking the question.
"No, sir, he went down shepherding in forty- three."

With acknowledgements to Frederick Forsyth.

I WONDER WHY

I've wondered why, I wonder why,
    We're born to live, and live to die;
The grass is green, and blue the sky,
      How can it be? I wonder why?

With joy and sadness, often we cry;
   How odd it is? I wonder why;
When problems strike we often sigh,
    Yet, does it help? I wonder why?

The birds fly in the high, free sky,
    Yet rodents, underground they lie;
When rain comes down, we wish it dry,
    When dry, we wish for rain. I wonder why?

When all is done, this wondering why,
    With thoughts that fires my mind to fly;
The mysteries close when it's time to die,
    As there's no need to wonder why.

LA BONNE VIE

Oh, hello Tracey, it must be years.
   Was it, I think, at your office dance;
With you so full of tears,
   Thinking that George was your very last chance.

I'll take you to Fortnum's for a nice cup of tea,
   And it will be lovely to chat about old times;
I thought it was you, or it might have been me,
   That saw Teddy stagger out of *The Limes*.

But, since those dull days in Goldarming,
   My life has been excitingly good;
With meeting new friends, all so charming,
   And with time I soon understood.

My first boyfriend, Hugh was at Harrow,
   And at his daddies estate I would stay;
But all that I heard was: "Are the pigs due to farrow?"
   So I decided to run and call it a day.

Now, Tracy, you would have adored my friend Fritz,
   A diplomat at the German embassy;
There's nothing he liked better than to dine at the Ritz,
   Not with anyone else, but just me.

I do think you would have adored my dear Freddie,
    We were always laughing, just two reckless fools;
If you remember he was a friend of Teddy,
    And we denied deliciously at Rules.

And Tracy, with all of life's ups and downs,
    I always think it very nice;
To breakfast with my friends at Brown's,
    As this gives each day that little extra spice.

I get all my shoes and handbags at boutiques,
    Just where else could one have such fun?
But, when one needs a champagne, it's just Harvey Nich's,
    In the bar, where you meet just everyone.

Now, my poor Charles seems always so fraught,
    As bankers seem always to be;
So to calm him down, we dine at the Connaught;
    A wonderful time, Just my dear Charles and me.

But I must tell you Tracy, life is not all Claridge's,
    There are times when one just loses ones senses;
It's really not all limousines and hackney carriages.
    But, I must be off now, and let you get back to your
    Marks and Spencer's.

LOVE IN MAY

The eager buds unfold in May,
 As spring flowers wave their goodbye;
It is but little we have to pay,
    For this floral splendor, bright and gay.

As morning rose out of the shadows,
  The clouds go floating by;
Casting their shade over the green meadows,
    As April's showers will surely die.

I met my love, who was born of May,
  Her presence blossomed as the flower;
Her heart was warm, and dare I say:
    I loved her more at every hour.

Flowers of love and love of flowers,
  May has brought us close together;
Such beauty, joy and love, all is ours,
    Until that cold sunset hour calls forever.

CRICKHOWEL

Lying below the beautiful hills of the Brecons,
    The sleepy old town of Crickhowel jogs along;
With the river Usk, that always beckons,
    In summer showers and sweet bird song.

Where a great mound stands beside the town,
    A Norman castle stood and told of many tales;
Where Glendower, in the fifteenth century brought it down,
    In his final bid for the independence of Wales.

I remember now, when I was young and fleet,
    Walking through the tufted grass and plantations;
And smelling the dew dropped meadowsweet,
    Wandering with unrivalled joy at God's creations.

One early morning I set out alone,
    To discover a gentle walk, a friend had told;
Across the thirteen arched bridge of stone,
    Past Legar Lodge, into a cattle fold.

And, gently, with my surprised eyes seeking,
    All that I could to fill my heart with pleasure;
With every step, my memory keeping,
    Of the Welsh landscape now at my leisure.

I now wander slowly past an ancient farm,
 Where dogs are barking so alert;
And hoping that they would do me no harm,
 As indeed I would not give them hurt.

Escaping from my fear of canine anger,
 I reach a canal through the plantation's ridges;
And, now, with tranquil thoughts of leaving danger,
 I pass under some three or four bridges.

Now leaving the canal and pleasure boats behind,
 I walk down the lane to St Catwg's church;
And in Llangattocks church, what should I find?
 But stocks and whipping posts, without a search.

And, now, in the autumn of my life, so long,
 With the memory of that day so clear;
With the joys of countryside and birds' sweet song,
 In that small, heavenly patch of yesteryear.

REQUIEM

I see you now on Durdham Down,
   Young and fleet - just running along;
     Tugging at my hand without a sound,
      But, yet my head was full of song.

Those were the days when life was young,
   Where joy and living would never end;
     But the distant bells of war were rung,
      And what in life will that message bring?

With fond goodbyes and our sad tears,
   For so long parted we know not when;
     Just living those long days, with hopes and fears,
      Clinging to life as the gentle wren.

My love went to sleep in a foreign land,
   Without goodbyes he fell down;
     And I was not there to hold his hand,
      Yet I see him still on Durdham Down.

GABRIELLA

How can I describe the ukulele lady?
  Who fills our world with so much fun;
Her joy abounds when days are shady,
    Goodbye clouds, and welcome to the sun.

It was by chance that I first discovered,
  The ukulele lady at an undertaker's dinner;
Where their practiced, solemn faces truly hovered,
    Then brought to life and laughter with this winner.

With songs recalled from the music hall,
  George Formby is the star;
But Polish folk-songs are, to us all,
    Her greatest charm by far.

How sweet the sound of tinkling strings,
  In their staccato notes of pure delight;
A melody borne on quivering wings,
  That warms the heart through dark and light.

The Polish blood runs through their veins,
  Like streams of running gold;
As kindness and joy forever reigns,
  Where her love of life truly enfolds.

She is that soul, just full of life,
    That stretches out with love and care;
Little matter her battles with grief and strife,
    Her presence and love shines everywhere.

THOUGH WINTER CAME

Though winter came, stealing the autumn sun,
  I walked the boundless woods of Wyre.

Where serried ranks of pines are called to order,
    By some forgotten power and melting together,
    In an endless canvas of green.

Their branches waving a baton to a symphony,
  Of nature in the winds changing rhythms and now;
    The trees of a broader girth join this orchestra,
    Their naked limbs teasing the wind.

Then through a stolen gap I saw a sun-drenched,
  Snow-painted level, blinding the birds in flight.

And, once more in the wood the twigs and branches are,
  Bed-steading down, holding the leaves in a patchwork;
    Of quilting reverence.

Two lovers are wrapped together, embracing the wind,
  As dusk hides their dreams.

The silent earth is listening helplessly to the,
  Footsteps of mankind.

And, on this earth, the cones and needles come floating,
  Down, weaving a carpet for the padding, moonlit, dappled;
    Foxes and badgers snuffling, and worming down to their
    Earth-worked setts.

Now, once more this winter's day is closing,
    In that tranquility only night can give.

MISSPENT YOUTH

When I was in my youth, just then,
   Where lilacs marked my home,
And loving parents were asking: "When
    Are you getting off the phone?"

Struggling with my studies, in my room,
   But thinking naughty thoughts of girls;
While listening to a rock band tune,
    Regardless just how loud the record whirls.

Just why I didn't make the choice
   To go to Uni far from home;
Where I could have a single voice,
    Not "No", or "Yes, Mother" - just "Leave me alone".

My parents I just love to bits,
   But they don't understand;
That a guy like me adores the hits,
    Of the latest all-girls band.

Now as my room adorns a wall,
   With some topless glamour girls;
My mother thinks it's too close to call,
    As her obvious distaste unfurls.

Of course, my Dad's a proper guy,
    He thinks the birds are great;
"But, just don't tell your mother,
    Which would give her more to hate."

My God - I wished I was at Uni,
    Living here is such a bore;
"Do this, do that," is all I hear,
    Until my head becomes one big sore.

But, had I made Uni as my home,
    No cups of tea in bed each morning;
No dinners or free telephone,
    Just this easy life and free to roam.

MORNING SHIFT

The morning mist was lingering in pools of white,
  As the village became no more;
As small damp beads caressed my face,
  Cooling the day's ambitions.

I must unlock the gates and garage doors,
  Before the customers arrive.

The morning moon is greeting the sun,
  Hiding the stars. And all is calm as Monday.

I must raise the jack and remove,
  The handbrake cable.

How beautiful hang the clouds scudding,
  Across the sky, as limpid pools reflect;
    Their unchallenged chase.

Check the lights -I see the offside rear,
  Needs replacing.

A silent breeze brushes itself along,
  Carrying the sweet smell of June roses,
    Carelessly planted. But, now their perfume
      Is all forgiveness.

The exhaust pipe looks shot at and the,
Customer won't like the cost of a new one.

Suddenly, the sky becomes as grey
   As the Squirrel that invades our day, stealing the nuts;
     Offered to the birds,
       And leaping and jumping
         To shelter from the threatening rain.

The cylinder head gasket is cracked and,
  Must be replaced with a new one.

As the rain came down, thunder and lightning
   Played among the clouds. The dogs were barking,
 Filling the vacuum created by the silence of the birds,
And the corrugated tin roof played a Chopin prelude.

  Must track the front wheels before I take,
  This one on a road test.

As quickly as it came, the rain parted the clouds,
   And the sun brazened down onto the wet street and,
All is calm, as suddenly a melody of,
Birdsong filled the air and all is peace in my world.

What a busy day- I'll be happy to get back home and relax.

Each and every day is full of surprises with the rain,
Competing with the sun and the clouds in the reckless;
Adventures, call them together. Ordering our days and
Nights in a fantasy, giving life to precious England.

AN UNINVITED GUEST

Isn't it lovely - just the two of us alone,
In our cosy home, with a nice cup of tea;
And enjoying a hot, buttered scone,
A quiet afternoon; just you and me.

Since we're now older, with time on our hands,
Just being together is always a treat;
Thinking and talking of those foreign lands,
That we enjoyed so much, together - my Sweet.

Oh, dear - someone's coming through our garden gate.
I think it's your sister, Hilda. I'd better open the door;
We just can't pretend that we're out - it's too late.
We're in for some pain - she's such a great bore.

Well, hello Hilda. What a surprise seeing you,
We do hope that you are keeping well;
"I'm not bad at all, except I've just had the flu,
And my usual problem with my ankles that swell.

I think I should tell you about our baby sister Gertie,
If you remember, she married Charlie Walker;
And he, God bless him, can't help getting shirty,
'Cause, can you believe it, Rose is pregnant - his precious
daughter.

I'm sure I mustn't bore you with all of my affairs,
    But I thought that you should know;
That I fell down the two bottom stairs,
    And what do you think - I broke my big toe.

Oh I almost forgot to tell you about Gertie's curtains,
    That she had made, that go right down to the floor:
She said that she should have had them before – she's certain,
    And that they look so much better than the short ones
    before.

Well I'll have to be off now. It's been so nice seeing you.
    Cheerio, Hilda. We're so glad that you came;
Oh, my darling, just how did we get through,
    All that dribble, that could drive us insane!

MOTHERLAND

I leaned upon the broken style,
  With silken cobwebs, dancing in the breeze,
    On this dew-dropped morning's smile.

Land spreading is challenged by the sky,
    The scudding clouds hiding the sun,
      With willows bending with a gentle sigh.

Grasses are hiding the orchids waking to the sun,
  With bees fumbling the flowers untiring,
    Until all their pollen is now won.

My feet springing to the beating of my heart,
  Are cushioned by the grass,
    As white-tailed rabbits stop and start.

Lazy as the cows, with their backs to the breeze,
  Listen to the fluting of the birds,
    As summer puts the world at ease.

Pebbles are now skittering, as the stream does flow,
  As I hear the rippling water,
    And then a sudden splash reveals a water vole.

The tumbling, swirling stream now joins the river falls,
    Where chub and barbel rule,
      And all is well as Mother Nature calls.

Then looking now where woodland masks the sky,
As squirrels hide their nuts in grass,
And, in this joy and wonderment, I cry.

COMPANIONSHIP

Love is forever, and never dies,
  And rules our very being;
It's a companionship that never lies,
  With our hearts forever seeing;
Ways to cherish, ways to love,
  As the silent wings of a heavenly dove.

Two people, bound in love forever,
  Share each other's thoughts;
And live a life, just two together,
  With treasured times and with all sorts;
Of forgiving and forgetting,
  With companionship un-letting.

With those of us who live alone,
  And needing friendships sharing;
Just that call that makes this home,
  Once more, with those so caring;
And, so the light shines, tapping,
  Into friends and neighbours, laughing.

Walking through the land so green,
  With flowers, grasses and sunlit boughs;
Is giving life to me unseen,
  Delighting with the sheep and cows;
This companionship is in God's fresh air,
  Floating with the clouds, without care.

SEESAW

Out of the way and off to his work,
   So I'll have a nice cup of tea;
Before I have to start ironing his shirt,
   Just how would he do without me?

I'll call my friend Alice - we both need a chat
   About her husband's shocking affair;
How could he do it to poor Alice?
     And that female's only fit to say: "Come upstairs".

There's two weeks of laundry I must get done,
   A housewife's life is all chores;
I'd much rather be out in the sun,
   Than be chained like this and indoors.

"Well, hello Alice, I'm glad you've come round,
   There's so much to talk about now;
For, in Jack's pocket, just see what I've found!
   Stop blushing Alice, and we don't want a row."

"I think we'd both better have a coffee and cake,
   As there's some explaining to do;
As the bra in Jack's pocket is your favourite make,
   Which seems a real how do you do."

"But, Alice, I've a confession to make,
 I'm that female, and I can't make an excuse.
And to admit, dear Alice - it's never too late -
 That I have been seeing your Bruce."

THIS PRECIOUS PLOT

Daybreak comes each day to charm,
    With morning mists their curtain down;
And early houses are silent as good bye,
    With all the fields as green as envy.

The cotton-wooling clouds are chasing the sun,
    Over hedgerows their geometric patterns run;
With landscaped, scattered trees to clean the air,
    And roads and lanes signposted to everywhere.

Farmyard animals think free, in their field-fenced jails,
    Below, the slender trees, braving the gales;
As rains are washing and feeding the land,
        With nature commanding every strand.

Country gardens are vegetating to man's hand,
        As needs of man and beast do understand;
Then, toils and patience always knows,
    That we must husband all that nature grows.

A blue and limpid lake below the lea
    Feeds streams and rivers to the sea;
Its gently rippling waves, pebbling to the shore,
    Brings life to Earth's verdant floor.

When evening comes, the birdsong keeps,
　And all is peace as nature sleeps;
The night a myriad of stars,
　And all is silent in these darkened hours.

WORCESTERSHIRE

Good to be in Worcestershire now that summer's here,
  With all the joys of town and country near;
With sedate Malvern with its blue remembered hills,
   Looking down to Hereford and Gloucestershire.

Take any lane that will lead to some delightful place,
   Whether it be among the orchards or some industrial race;
And, think, just once again of all that one can see,
   In this great county's timeless variety.

The river Severn slowly tumbling to the sea,
  Has witnessed every change in our history;
In this small county, that England made,
   A garden that man and nature now has laid.

The villages and towns are but jewels in the landscape,
   That toiling man and family go happily to escape;
In Worcestershire's ever changing and verdant bowers,
   That all can see the glory - that is ours.

That great landmark of placid Bredon Hill,
  Looks down on Cathedral and spires, and will;
See Evesham, Pershore, Mendips and the Malverns still,
   And, further onward Shropshire's Wrekin Hill.

The northern hills of Clee compete with Bredon's views:
    With sights of Dudley on the Penine slopes, which used;
To smelt the iron and mine the coal to fain,
    Which gave the Black Country its certain name.

Lying among the hills and valleys is the Forest of Wyre,
    With serried ranks of pine and broadleaf to admire;
And what more could be told of Worcestershire,
    This precious plot in England's golden shire.

THE BRICK'S STORY

My life began fired, in a brickyard's womb,
    Out of Earth's golden clay and rushing water;
Might I be moulded into a precious tomb,
    Or a dark blue son, or golden daughter.

In my first waking hour, cosied with my friends,
    I see myself rustic in the melting sun;
And I am that golden daughter, which lends
    A warmth and softness for everyone.

I am put to rest in the brickyard crèche,
    To stay a while, 'til my future's known;
Where they will give me a life that's fresh -
    Safe and sure, in a loving home.

One morning, as the sun was shining brightly,
    Strong hands took me away - I know not where;
Fearing a bruise, I held on tightly,
    And went to my new home, fine and fair.

Oh, the noise - the shouting, the talking and joking
    Lifted my heart - a happy place to dwell;
And, here I will stay, in the town of Woking,
    A library brick, I'm proud to tell.

I wonder why, and for what good reason,
   They might place me at some great height;
Seeing the changing days and seasons,
    Which might well give me some delight.

But, for me, it would be rather nice,
   Spending my days beside the door;
Which would give life that extra spice;
    Just meeting people would never be a bore.

The day has come - finished, the door ajar,
    With the bejewelled Mayor and Corporation;
Cutting the tape with pride, to near and far,
    To rousing cheers of joy and acclamation.

But, one dark night, when the day was spent,
   A stranger stopped as if by an open well;
As the water splashed, then the stranger went,
    I could have cried out loud, but would blush to tell!

Myself and all of my brickyard friends,
     Are settled now in a worthy place;
Lending ourselves, as this place intends,
    Welcoming readers with a smiling face.

VALHALLA

When often in my dreams of you, yet sleeping,
   Plucked from my quivering heart and jealous keeping;
Those eyes - those eyes, how deeply, blindly meeting,
   As waking light, the vision's sudden haste retreating.

Not long in this, our world that ugly, idle life,
   When, everything that's slaved for ends in strife;
The waking hours, to honour are but all to try,
   Away, far away, to Valhalla I would fly.

Now, in my modest house, where long, long hours I gave.
   Thoughts that are far and closing, with all to save;
My heart longing filled, I see before me, lie my sweetheart,
   And, here now, fresh mists spread her fragrance to my heart.

Yet, should I, need I – fly to Valhalla, when in this dark -
   A ray of life before me spreading as the lark;
Her ascending song and flutter of tiny wings,
   And living, just once more what new life brings.

MEMOIRE DE LA VIE

Now, thinking of this long, long life, reflecting,
    When others' rocks and boulders blocked my way;
I visited the myriad nooks and crevices, expecting,
    All before me: shifting sands; the toiling day.

My apprehension lives on in me, like some hidden dust,
    And I fly through all the memories, running short;
But, past the prickly stubble - the empty streams; the rust,
    The circle of those long years is now caught.

Now in, the rights of equals matures the essence,
    Like the perfections of all the heavens and Earth;
As the grand piano, blazed with its own cadence,
    And the nightingale on the bush, in happy mirth.

But, yet, for me there brightly shines your face alone,
    Just how fine - this world; a happy man I stand;
You are that life I loved to play and roam,
      You are the skylark singing over the land.

ARS LONGA VITA BREVIS

Time expanding; time diminishing - our chosen right,
    As art, in all its myriad forms, is living still;
And early cave paintings, to the present day,
    Are enchanting us with their delight.

There is not one picture in this our world,
    Be it by a royal portrait painter, or an eager child;
That does not for that someone be an important moment,
    In their life, where deep emotions are unfurled.

The hills around me are leaning on my window sill,
    As the landscape calls to me the poetry of life;
Where are those creations, of which we see but few,
    All captured in those countless watercolours still.

Artists are bound together to express their souls,
    To understand their wonder and satisfaction of life;
Even now, when some paintings look just as well upside-down,
    There is some obscure jargon to support their doubtful roles.

What more is there in art if not to entertain,
    In all the world's galleries of great renown;
And also countless ones in our local towns,
    Where art historians and critics make their name.

Though life is short, art is unchanging -
    Capturing that very moment, or just giving a voice;
Art, in all its forms, is there and enduring,
    While life, in its brief span, has little remaining.

A DAY TO REMEMBER

My love for you, sweet Earth, my mother,
      And golden dreams, and light and bliss;
This is the day I shall remember,
    Pellucid, crystal clear, like no other.

Summer, how pure the air, how clear the sky,
      With dewdrops fallen in the morning;
The weeping willows whispering o'er the river,
      And looking now to heaven, here I lie.

There is not one hour this day of awesome wonder,
    That I make haste to look into your lovely face;
You have made me happy, eager to live,
    For you, this day, remembering - nought asunder.

Your love is fragrant now, more deeply felt,
    Filling me with warmth and tender yearning;
And, now, I hear your gentle voice, and feel your rapid breath,
    This is a day to remember that life to me has dealt.

HILL CHORLTON, STAFFORDSHIRE

In a country village, where my life began,
   Where two lilac trees announced my home;
By a kind of meadowland a small stream ran,
   Where as a child I used to roam.

A meadow path, dappled and sunshine blinded,
   Would be my adventure along the way;
And I would stop and look, when I was minded,
   To everything that would fill my lovely day.

Then, here I stopped to eat a snack, with eager glee,
   Sitting there with a new found friend;
A robin, that danced to tease a crumb from me,
   Sharing my joy that all the world could lend.

Now, all these long years after, I stole away,
   To this village that was once my home;
And long to see, on this remembered day,
   The changes where I used to roam.

The meadow's there; the lambs, the sheep,
   The Windy arbor, where I used to play;
With those hidden treasures, that I'll always keep,
   Locked in my mind, 'til my closing day.

MARGARET

How should I, in this poor poet's hand,
    Write of a love, a life, a treasure;
A sapling tree, planted in my heart and hand,
    Stretching up to heaven with silent pleasure.

You are the early blossoms in the month of May,
    The mornings rising out of the dark;
You are the garden's scents - so warm, so gay,
    And the sweetest love song of the lark.

The martins scream. With song, the red-breast flies,
    As elms are sighing lightly, and slowly bend;
And, in my hand, your bosom, like the universe quiet lies,
    When all is peace, as any heartaches slowly mend.

You are the light which guides me through life's mists,
    And the winnowed grain, taken when the harvest's won;
You are the heart and soul that life has kissed,
    And I love you, with all that was, and all that is yet to come.

You light my life - blazing up in ardent heat,
    You are the limpid pool from the depths of ages;
With all the joys and hardships, ours to keep,
    In the book of life, written in its endless pages.

VIEW FROM MY STUDIO WINDOW

It is winter now and the view is still,
>   And I see the forest creep upon my village home:
Low skies hiding the distant tree-lined hill,
>   Wondrous peace and calm of nature, all alone.

Then, after dawn, I greet the stinging cold,
>   As midday hangs over Carrion Crow Hill;
And, now the river reflects blue, as clouds unfold,
>   And smoke flies high over Skeet's Farm still.

Across the Severn, at Meadow Lane,
>   The steam railway sounds another year;
And calm nature breathing her fragrance once again,
>   Where the fresh green grass grows near.

The forest path, with mottled sunshine blended,
>   Is greener now - not just an outline of the hills;
Yes, spring is here, with winter truly ended,
>   And the high, free sky with splendour thrills.

The meadow, now, is fresh as snow in sunshine,
>   As lambs leap and frolic to their mother's cry;
I stand in quiet solitude. The world is fine,
>   As I see a cormorant spread its wings to dry.

Late summer now as blue dragonflies fly by,
    And this day just trembled as if a leaf;
Such beauty is translucent; "Thank you, God" I cry,
    As autumn colours change into a golden wreath.

The morning sky in blazing red is shown,
    With dawn's crimson edging burns and tones;
While rustling leaves, the branches no longer stay,
    And soon, limned naked, all will stand alone.

RAIN

The world is ours, where no secrets hide,
   Where nature rules, with both joy and pain;
As man, with all his science, has but tried,
    To harness, at his will, the falling rain.

Our rivers and gentle streams but little know,
   While dancing and rippling, as if just a game;
As, blindly meandering through our land they go,
   But, would all be nought, without the precious rain.

Fall softly, rain, over all the nations,
   To fill the lakes and quench the thirsty land;
Preserve for the unborn future generations,
   This precious gift, bestowed by that unknown hand.

In its many moods the rain does surprise us still,
   With tempestuous flooding over the land;
But, yet more gently, warmly, by its own will,
   Gives life that nurtures all our needs to hand.

The distant rain can display a wondrous rainbow,
   But, when nearer still hides the landscape's view;
And, with all its variations, that we ought to know,
   The rain will surprise us with something new.

LOVE

Love has its words, and words cannot die:
    I love you, keep you and hold you in my arms;
You, it is, that is melting the clouds in the sky,
    Your perfect shape, perfumed hair and endless charms.

It's night, and alone, with the Severn sparking smoothly,
    While we are both passionate and pure;
Then, suddenly, I am awake, warm and dreamily,
    With my arms around you, safe and sure.

I see your eyes again, through the morning light,
    As dewdrops seem to fall, as we must part;
With memories floating alone, no shadow in sight,
    And my steadfast gaze, penetrating your heart.

One look at your sad face would bring my tears,
    As I go on and on, lost within my dreams;
The thought of losing you would mould my fears,
    But dreams do haunt me now it seems.

Now, gently waking from my torpid sleep,
    I know in my heart that life well's in delight;
And I feel your trembling hands in mine to keep,
    As our love is touched by golden moonlight.

The dawn's blazing morning light lights her face,
    And flowers spread their fragrance everywhere,
As I watch her movements full of grace,
    And listen to her voice, gentle and sincere.

To see her now fills my heart with warmth and fire,
    As lips meet lips, with fingers clasping fingers;
You are all my love and all my desire,
    And when she leaves, her perfumed presence lingers.

THOUGHTS OF AN ART STUDENT

When we were young artists, making our way,
    So carefree, ambitious, and so gay;
Different to the world, as others knew,
    Living lives so freely, our very few.

We studied long, with inspirations from the past,
    But, thinking figurative art could not last;
And lived, and truly loved, our lives together,
    Thinking a broader canvas would be ours forever.

Yet, somehow, as the months passed by,
    We heard the lectures, and we would try;
Moulding our minds in a structured way,
    Exploring old masters, as if in their day.

Was it without knowing, we were being tamed?
    Where confusion and ambition, we thought, constrained.
And were our abstract thoughts just being lost,
    With our self-expression dimmed or lost.

However, time and learning has prised us apart,
    Displaying our thoughts in individual art;
Not soulless clones, but to ourselves,
    In a world of art that our canvas tells.

MUCH TOO OLD

When thoughts go drifting through my mind,
  For this and that and every kind;
    I'm much too old for that.

I remember, in the days of yore,
    I was so happy on a cycle tour;
  But I'm much too old for that.

Why didn't I go waltzing and making love?
    But, for goodness sake, and heavens above;
  I'm much too old for that.

They said I could fly to Spain in a big aeroplane,
But do they think that I'm quite insane?
  I'm much too old for that.

My friends took me on a country ramble,
    But I would have preferred a motorcycle scramble;
  But I'm much too old for that.

They tell that life's not complete without *it*,
  But I tell you now, it's not for me;
    I'm much too old for that.

Perhaps whist, drive, and tea at the village hall
Would suit me quite well after all;
  As I'm not too old for that.

HOC OPUS, HIC LABOR EST

ABOUT THE AUTHOR

Dr Norman AJ Berisford as well as being a poet, is a world renowned expert in architectural science.

His first, co-authored book: A History of Interior Design, although published in 1983, is still recognised as one of the leading manuals on the physical and psychological aspects of interior lighting.

Norman is also an accomplished visual artist, specialising in water colours and has had many of his paintings exhibited and sold at auction. Although, he has always donated the proceeds to charity.

Norman says that he originally began writing poetry in his spare time as a way to relax, but it soon became a passion. This is the first time his complete poetry, which he describes as being a mixture of the sublime to whimsical, has ever been published.

He shares his life with Margaret, his wife at his home in Worcestershire.

ABOUT THE PUBLISHER

L.R. Price Publications is dedicated to publishing books by unknown authors.

We use a mixture of both traditional and modern publishing options to bring our authors' words to the wider world.

We print, publish, distribute and market books in a variety of formats including paper and hard back, electronic books e-books, digital audio books and online.

If you are, an author interested in getting your book published; or a book retailer interested in selling our books, please contact us.

www.lrpricepublications.com

L.R. Price Publications Ltd,
27 Old Gloucester Street,
London,
WC1N 3AX.

(0208) 1449188

publishing@lrprice.com

www.ingramcontent.com/pod-product-compliance
Lightning Source LLC
Chambersburg PA
CBHW071018040426
42443CB00007B/837